DOS AND DON'TS WHEN YOU'VE BEEN DUMPED

VIRGINIA KATHLEEN BOYD

Westfeld Press
HUDSON, OHIO

Copyright © 2019 by Virginia Kathleen Boyd.

All rights reserved. No part of this publication may be reproduced, distributed or transmitted in any form or by any means, including photocopying, recording, or other electronic or mechanical methods, without the prior written permission of the publisher, except in the case of brief quotations embodied in critical reviews and certain other noncommercial uses permitted by copyright law. For permission requests, write to the publisher, addressed "Attention: Permissions Coordinator," at the address below.

Inquiries to SOS Seminars, Inc., P.O. Box 493
Aurora, Ohio 44202

V.K. Boyd/Westfeld Press
Hudson, Ohio

Book Layout ©2013 BookDesignTemplates.com

Ordering Information:
Quantity sales. Special discounts are available on quantity purchases by corporations, associations, and others. For details, contact the "Special Sales Department" at the address above.

Dos and Don'ts When You've Been Dumped/ Virginia Kathleen Boyd. -- 1st ed.
ISBN 978-0-9916173-8-8

PREFACE

Being dumped is devastating and humiliating, and one of the most demeaning experiences that can happen to anyone. Along the way, many of us have lost someone we loved, or thought we loved, to somebody else.

Maybe it was a high-school sweetheart, maybe it was someone we thought we loved, but who only considered us a friend. When we realized that we had lost that "one true love", and that person was not interested in us anymore (or maybe never), we felt embarrassed, and in many ways, ashamed.

But over time, we got over that embarrassment, and we moved along in our lives, and eventually we did find a real true love. We got married, had a family, and lived happily ever after. Sound familiar? Maybe this was YOU.

If it was, you might have gone a long (or short) way in your married life thinking that you were still the ONE. You had built your life with this person, and, for the most part, you were happy and content.

Then a day came that changed everything forever!!!

What happened? Let's take a closer look.

You have been told, or you have learned, that your partner does not love you, has never loved you, is moving out, has been unfaithful, or tells you any one of a number of other crushing facts or reasons for why IT IS OVER. You find yourself sitting in the rubble of what may be the biggest shock of your life, and you don't know what to do next.

Where do you begin to rebuild this relationship? Do you kick the bum out? Do you forgive him? Do you jump off the nearest bridge? Is it possible to just start over, and if so how? Are you so frozen in place, that you cannot take even one step in any direction?

These are serious questions that will occupy your life, both night and day, for much of the foreseeable future. Right now, your mind is racing wildly from belief to disbelief–and you haven't any idea of what to do or how to do it.

Before doing ANYTHING, please take a moment to deliberately do NOTHING. Take a moment (or a day or a week) to just stop and think. Take some real time to consider the impact of whatever actions you do (and will) take, and please also consider some alternatives that may be open to you before you do ANYTHING else.

Right now, you may feel that your world has just collapsed around you, and maybe life is not even worth living. Please realize that you are a special and valuable person and that YOU HAVE RIGHTS and that YOU

Dos and Don'ts When You've Been Dumped

HAVE CHOICES. It is up to you to exercise any and all your choices and options to achieve the best possible outcome in the worst possible situation.

Please read on **IF YOU NEED HELP RIGHT NOW** !!!

TABLE OF CONTENTS:

1. DON'T - OWN SOMEONE ELSE'S BAD BEHAVIOR!!! 1

2. DO – GIVE YOURSELF 90 DAYS TO RECOVER 9

3. DON'T - GIVE UP THE MORAL HIGH GROUND.......... 15

4. DO - TAKE A THOROUGH INVENTORY...................... 23

5. DON'T - DO ANYTHING DRASTIC!!!........................... 29

6. DO - KNOW YOUR OPTIONS... 35

7. DON'T - GET EVEN.. 39

8. DO - BE KIND - IT'S GOOD FOR YOU......................... 45

9. DON'T - SIGN ANYTHING!!!.. 49

10. DO - BE OKAY (FOR YOU AND YOUR CHILDREN)... 55

11. DON'T - LET IT EVER HAPPEN AGAIN....................... 59

12. DO - BE PREPARED FOR YOUR MARRIAGE TO WORK!!!
....63

Note: This book is written from the perspective of a married wife, but information herein may also be useful for husbands or for anyone who is suffering from an unexpected or unwanted breakup.

ONE

DON'T

OWN SOMEONE ELSE'S BAD BEHAVIOR!!!

If you just learned that he is leaving, you may think that you need to act fast. You think that you must stop him from going out that door. If he leaves, he will be forever lost to you. Are you searching your mind for some way to make him understand how much you love him? What can you do to make him change his mind?

After all, he has told you that this is ALL YOUR FAULT, and you are thinking that you must do something fast to fix what you have obviously broken.

STOP RIGHT HERE!!

If that is what you have been told, or if that is what you are thinking, then you may have been **tricked.** Think about it for a moment. Has he been telling you all along that he is not happy? Has he asked for you to join him in counseling? Has he invited you on a vacation to re-energize your marriage? What was it that made him not love you? What exactly have you done—or not done?

If your recent history is standard "couple" life—you were just living your lives—maybe been together 3, 5, 10, 15 years, (or more)—and all along you were content, and thought he was content, and then suddenly you learned that it is over, don't be too quick to blame yourself. The fault may not be YOURS.

Sure, things haven't always been perfect. You have made mistakes, and he has made mistakes. Nobody is perfect.

You have, however, always found a way to fix your differences. You have always mended your fences, made up, and continued with your lives and your relationship.

Now suddenly, you find that he has been keeping track of all your mistakes, and has been adding them up, like an itemized bill, and he has presented you with that bill asking for payment in full. Somehow, no matter what you do or say, you do not seem to have the resources that he is demanding for you to "pay up" and to go on in your relationship. Somehow, you have failed what seems like a final exam, and you are being expelled. And to top it off, you are being blamed (condemned really) to be the one who has ruined your own family, and who has spoiled everything for everyone.

Dos and Don'ts When You've Been Dumped

That is the **trick**. You are being abandoned and dumped by someone who is unwilling to accept responsibility for HIS decision. Instead he is trying to force YOU to be the one to bear the burden, (maybe for the rest of your life), of a dark cloud of REGRET hanging over your head. He is tricking you into being the one to bear the blame. He has blamed you for ruining everything. He has condemned you as being both UNFORGIVEN and UNFORGIVABLE.

This is the worst kind of cruelty. Placing his guilt and his blame on you is treason and betrayal, and if you permit it to stand, you will be forever shackled to a life of REGRET for both you and your children. You must not let this happen.

If this is what is going on in your relationship right now, you might be wondering, why is it important who gets the blame? Isn't it really all about getting him BACK? Why all the fuss about regret, and why is regret so bad anyway? It doesn't seem like it should last forever–why would it?

You might be thinking right now how sick you are over what he said that you have done–of all the mistakes you made. You might not be able to bear to have him leave you without telling him how sorry you are. Maybe he will change his mind and stay if he sees that you are willing to change.

Please be aware that he WANTS the break up to be your fault so that he can be justified in LEAVING. He is not looking for a reason to STAY, but rather an excuse to GO, and you must not give him one.

Let's step back for a moment and think about our own past regrets. All of us can remember times in our lives when, if we had been one second earlier or later, we could have avoided an accident. If we had not spoken that one word, we might not have lost that job. If we had not missed that one phone call, we would have had some wonderful opportunity that went to another. Maybe we regret not speaking to a parent, and then losing that mother or father never having expressed our love.

Many people never recover from that kind of regret. We turn that regret over and over in our minds for weeks, months, even years. Sometimes it never leaves us.

So here you are now, having been told that you are the reason that you are being dumped. He is reminding you of all your mistakes, and how inadequate you are (and have always been). Instead of being a gift in his life, you are THE reason for all his unhappiness, and THE reason that he has decided to leave.

Please, please, please–DO NOT ACCEPT THE BLAME!!!

Please be advised that THIS IS A TRICK. It is an old trick, and it is used again and again. It is used because it works. It gets HIM off the HOOK!

Blaming you becomes his hall PASS. It becomes his rationale and his justification. It is his EXCUSE for doing the wrong thing, and making it seem like the right thing. He tells himself, his friends, your children, and the whole

Dos and Don'ts When You've Been Dumped

family, that he cannot love you, maybe that he never loved you. You were just too hard to live with, maybe too demanding, maybe just too unlovable.

He tells everyone that it isn't fair for the two of you to stay in a loveless marriage. He tells everyone, that he loves the kids, and this is best for THEM. Somehow, he is managing to dump you and your (his) family, and still be a stand-up guy.

And WORST OF ALL, you think you are losing this really swell STAND-UP guy.

Come on–let's get real. Let's think about that for a minute. If he were truly a stand-up guy, and if indeed he really has been unhappy for all this time, then why did he not stand up sooner, and ask for some help in working through all his despair and unhappiness.

It may be true that you could have gone out and done things together more often, maybe you could have lost weight, or kept the house neater. You are not claiming to be perfect. But Heaven knows there certainly were things he could have done to make the relationship better too.

If he really wanted a better relationship with YOU, he could have asked you for a date (maybe instead of other women)? He could have made it clear that he was struggling, or that he was unhappy, but he DID NOT.

Instead you both somehow just slipped into a comfortable lifestyle where you did some things your way and he did some things his way, and that was the arrangement. You never knew there was a big problem until now. He never let his unhappy secret out, and now, under all those circumstances, there should be no reason for you to bear the responsibility for this split. He has brought this upon himself. It was HIS decision.

End of sentence–end of story.

Whether he blames you or he has now convinced YOU to blame you, please be advised that you DO NOT NEED TO ACCEPT THIS BLAME.

The next time, he tries to lay responsibility for the breakup on you, just say "Please, don't insult my intelligence. YOU are the one abandoning me, and YOUR family. It is YOU who are doing the wrong thing, not I. I refuse to accept the blame for your bad behavior," and then just leave it there.

Don't try to explain–don't try to convince him. Just say it and walk away. It is the truth, and the truth can stand on its own merit.

That will put the blame squarely back where it belongs. You will have no guilt and no REGRETS for owning what really belongs to him–his bad behavior in making this shocking decision by himself and on his own–a decision that affects **everybody**.

By not owning the responsibility for what he has decided to do, you will experience a freedom from regret that nothing else will provide.

Sure, you will still be sad, you will cry, and be afraid, and have unhappy moments. But you will be able to concentrate on those things that you can and should do, rather than nurse the guilt that he has imposed on you for his own lack of commitment.

Dos and Don'ts When You've Been Dumped

This ONE STEP will take you weeks and months ahead in the healing process of this crisis, and it may be a building block for saving your relationship.

TWO

DO

GIVE YOURSELF NINETY DAYS TO RECOVER FROM THE SHOCK

There is a saying that "Time heals all Wounds". While time does put distance between us and a past-painful event, time does not make that bad experience disappear completely.

While time doesn't necessarily heal all wounds, it does seem that in cases were a relationship has been fractured, that after ninety days, the pain of the trigger event takes on more of a historical significance than it did as a current disaster. In many cases, an offended partner does feel better ninety days later than they did at the time of the break.

To make the point more clearly, right now, you should put an X on your calendar ninety days from today and use it as a target date and as a point to work towards hoping that when you get to that date, that you will feel a little better.

Life is filled with daily events, and as the days come and go over the next ninety days, other events will come and go in your life, and each one of them will impact you in different ways. Some days will be better than others, and while a break-up is a HUGE event, there will be other events to tend to along the way that will offer support and in some cases distraction from the pain of the break-up.

Remember that every event in our lives shapes us a little bit. Even the simple act of running into a friend on the street changes us. We hear news of a mutual friend, we share a story together, or we just encourage each other. Whatever it is, we change into a person just a little different than the person we were before.

Over a period of time all of these events gradually begin to mold our character and our being. Hopefully over time, we begin to mature and grow and become our better selves.

Don't expect to be healed however in ninety days. Time does not remove or "heal" those events, which were painful to us. Like having been cut, we can always see the scar that is left behind, and if we think about it, we can even remember the pain we felt at the time. After a long enough time though, we no longer feel the actual pain, and we must remind ourselves to even remember the cut.

That is a little like what will happen over the next ninety days. After many tears and sleepless nights, along with many zombie-like days, you will begin to develop a new reality in your life.

Life will never be what it was before, but ninety days out, life is not as tragic as it was the day you "found out". You have slowly begun to move forward and have begun to process the news from before.

If for today, you can decide that things will be better in ninety days, then maybe you can hang on today, and get through today.

What will have happened in ninety days you ask?

Well for one thing, you may discover that everything was a mistake, and he really didn't mean all the things he said. He will have had time to think over his behavior, and realize that he was out of line, and maybe he will have apologized and even returned.

Another thing that might happen, is that you realize that he has not been "with you" for a long time, and that you have been a doormat, a gopher, and a victim, and maybe you will not be quite so devastated after you have had time to think about all of that. You may begin to analyze your own feelings and needs and discover that he is the one who needs to shape up. You might not want to go on as you have been going all along.

You might discover also, that while you are still hurt, you now are thinking more rationally, and you can separate how you feel about the situation from how you feel about yourself. You might begin to feel less guilty and maybe a little more indignant or even a little angry at how you have been treated.

Also, within the next ninety days, you will have time to consider who to share your feelings with, and in whom you can confide. You will have an opportunity to get good advice from trusted friends or family members.

During that time, you may find out just who your friends really are, and who will stick with you. A true friend is someone who can be honest, but not hurtful. Friends are those people who edify each other. You should feel better about yourself after having been with a friend, not worse.

If you find that your friends are making you feel bad or guilty about your split-up, then you might want to move on to your other friends.

One bit of warning here - remember, that those people who know both you and your partner will undoubtedly have something to say about one or both of you. Please RESIST the urge to GOSSIP and carry personal stories about your partner. Remember that you can be trusted with a confidence, even if you don't trust him anymore, so make sure you remain your honorable self.

Do not take this opportunity to tell every one of your friends every bad thing you have ever thought about your partner. Remember he may want to come back, and you may want to take him back, so don't make him look like a total "jerk" to every person whom both of you know.

What should happen over this next 90 days is that you will gain information, encouragement, and support, and as you begin to dissect and categorize what you learn, you

Dos and Don'ts When You've Been Dumped

will begin to get a truer picture of what has happened in your relationship.

Unfortunately, you may also find yourself going to the unemployment office, looking for another place to live, looking for assistance, looking for a car, or any number of scary or uncomfortable experiences, and while these will not be the best moments of your life, they will serve as a distraction, and you may learn just how strong and capable you are, which will only serve to build your confidence.

Take the next ninety days–consider it a sabbatical–and learn to live in the day, even in the moment. Do not try to see into the future, and do not try to predict the outcome.

If you pick up your feet and walk one step at a time and live one day at a time, you will be pleasantly surprised to find that you have likely worked through many issues and will not be in the same state 90 days from now as you are today.

THREE

DON'T

GIVE UP THE MORAL HIGH GROUND

Out of desperation, it is easy to fall into the joint traps of either trying to make him jealous, or of overplaying your need to make yourself more desirable.

Following are some ideas that might come into your mind. If these are not part of your normal behavior, NOW IS NOT the time to begin experimenting.

DON'T GET PREGNANT TO TRY TO HANG ON TO HIM:

It may occur to you that he might not leave you if you are pregnant. Forget it. Getting pregnant to keep a man is

NEVER a good idea. First off, having a baby is a big decision. Being pregnant is a difficult time. Mothers need help and support during a pregnancy, and this is not the time that your partner is going to be there for you.

Additionally, after the baby arrives, you will have a new person in your life to feed and care for. You are already in a desperate situation, with your life in turmoil, and if you get pregnant now, once you come to your senses, you will realize how desperately you behaved, and you may end up having an abortion which is also not a good idea - regrettable for many.

If you have the baby, who will care for him when you are working? Will you have enough income to pay for a sitter for another child?

If you get pregnant, and you have difficulty in working, or caring for your child, you will find that you have given your partner a leg-up when it comes time for the courts to make child custody decisions. If you are not already pregnant, DO NOT GET PREGNANT NOW.

DON'T BECOME A SEX GODDESS:

Being sexy might seem like a good ploy to get your partner back but remember that much of his interest outside your home is in having a *new* relationship. He is not looking at you that way right now. Remember, he is trying to justify breaking up.

If you suddenly start wearing tight dresses or pants, low-cut tops, and short skirts, or clothes that are different than your normal attire, you will seem desperate to him, and he will think you are playing a game.

If you are trying to be sexy for others, to make your partner jealous, you might in fact get the attention of others, but do you want other men in your life, and in your home while you are trying to resurrect your relationship with your partner? The chance of this working is slim, but you may incite disagreement or violence in or near your children if your partner thinks HIS children are being threatened by your other men.

Such incidents can also be fodder in a custody hearing.

DON'T HAVE AN AFFAIR OR ONE-NIGHT STAND:

Whether or not you change your wardrobe style, you might consider an affair, or a one-night stand an effective way to get the attention of your partner.

Consider the example of one couple where the husband was inattentive to the wife, and she assumed that he had an outside lover. Whether or not he did, nobody knows, but she up and decided to have sex with a third party to let her partner see that she was desirable. Then she CONFESSED to him what she had done.

While the marriage had been languishing for years, as soon as the husband found out about the wife's infidelity, he packed up and left. He KNEW that his wife had been unfaithful, and that was all he needed. HE HAD THE MORAL HIGH GROUND, and he has been using it against her ever since.

And to make matters worse, she had no proof that he had done anything wrong, but HE DID have proof of what she had done. As a result, she had much less leverage in how the custody was handled regarding their daughter.

Don't Leave Home:

This is a very bad idea. You might think that if you run away from home, that your partner will be worried sick about what has happened to you and will be so happy to have you return that he will forget that he stopped loving you.

It doesn't work that way. If you do anything irrational, it will only confirm in his mind that you are desperate and needy, and it will drive him further away.

Also, please remember that if you leave home, that you will also be leaving your "stuff". It has taken years for you to build your life. You have years of memories in your things; special furniture, bedding, dishes, pictures, and many other personal and valuable belongings.

If you leave home, your partner can claim that you ABANDONED HIM, and he can claim ownership of some or much of the stuff that you left.

Please Note: If your life or safety is at risk in any way, it may be better to seek protective help. It could be dangerous to stay in a location where your partner is making threats of abuse to you or your children. If that is the case, good advice is to seek professional help.

Dos and Don'ts When You've Been Dumped

However, if you are just trying to shock your otherwise rational partner into becoming desperate for you, it will not work, and again, you will only give him good reason for leaving and/or divorcing you. Under rational circumstances, DO NOT RUN AWAY.

DON'T DRINK AND DON'T DO DRUGS:

There is not much good to say about this one. If you get drunk, or get high on drugs, you put your life and the lives of those who depend on you in great jeopardy.

If anyone sees you drunk or high, even ONE TIME, you have given your partner the MORAL HIGH GROUND, and he can claim that you are an unfit mother and use your behavior against you in court.

Even if your partner regularly drinks or takes drugs, do not think that you can mimic his behavior without repercussions. His bad behavior might be the root of the problem, but if you behave the same way, nobody will believe you, and he will have a weapon to use against you.

DON'T ALLOW HIM TO BRING OTHER WOMEN INTO YOUR HOME:

An odd thing happens sometimes when life begins to unravel. When people become irrational, they think of things they would have never considered before.

Occasionally, a spouse may look for an opportunity to bring another woman into his marriage in some way. Maybe he suggests giving a room in the house to a nice college student who is doing an internship at his office, which makes the wife uncomfortable with his relationship with this intern.

Maybe he suggests to his wife that their friends are enjoying an "open" marriage, and that their friends are having sex with other partners, trading partners, having group sex, or some other behavior that deviates from the norm and from the wife's comfort zone.

Maybe he is constantly checking on a friend or neighbor to make sure that she has groceries, or is mowing her lawn, or running her errands.

Whatever it is, you suddenly realize that you and your husband are not alone anymore.

If you find that this is happening to you, trust your good judgment and put an end to it. Even though he seems to be in better spirits and is happier with YOU when you "play along" with this arrangement, please resist the urge to compromise your good value system. Under no circumstances should there be anyone else in your house or bed but you and him and he should not be in anyone else's house or bed.

He is not likely to spring this on you suddenly. He will more likely begin to finesse the subject with you to see your reaction.

Whatever it is that he is suggesting, if it involves another woman (or another man), or any arrangement that makes you uncomfortable, just say "No thanks–I am not interested!!!"

Dos and Don'ts When You've Been Dumped

Don't even entertain the thought. Remember, this is another trick. If you do anything deviant, or if you give your permission for him to do anything outside of your marriage, it will be used against YOU later in court.

Again, remember to maintain the high moral ground. You will not need to explain anything to anyone later.

FOUR

DO

TAKE A THOROUGH INVENTORY

Sometimes we behave in ways that we would find unacceptable if we observed that behavior in others. Consider the case where an observer described the following event:

"One day at the supermarket, I noticed a couple with a small child shopping for groceries. The wife was yanking at the arm of the child, and barking orders at the husband, and basically making a scene. The husband looked around embarrassed and shot his wife dirty looks when she would look away. It was very uncomfortable, and she was clearly embarrassing everybody without realizing how much her husband hated it."

This kind of behavior happens all the time. People often have a tendency to slip into their own world of chores, pressures, and deadlines, and fail to realize that everyone around them may not be on the same frequency.

It is easy to have a relationship get lost in the shuffle. Maybe your partner has been feeling this way, or maybe there have been other things that you have done to turn your partner against you. Here now you have been yanked up by a chain to realize that you have a problem, and you must step back and evaluate where it began, and more importantly, how serious it is.

STEP BACK:

Stepping back means that you should try to go back in time and try to remember when you began to feel that you and your partner first became distant and disengaged from one another.

Was there a time when he began to complain about the way you cleaned the house, did the laundry, cooked, or maybe how you took care of yourself.

Those comments, while they might have been off-handed to you, were probably serious clues to how your partner had begun to feel. He may have been sending you smoke signals without being straightforward and direct.

Sometimes partners are afraid to broach a subject for fear of antagonizing their partner, and instead begin perpetual complaining about peripheral issues.

Dos and Don'ts When You've Been Dumped

Instead of saying, "Honey, I am not happy right now, and I have not been happy for a long time. Please sit down and let's talk over some of the things that would help to make me more engaged in our relationship and in you". He may instead have said something like, "You should lay off the groceries for a little while." That of course did not endear him to you, and made you angry, and you probably ate more. In that case, neither of you did the helpful things that would have improved your relationship.

If you remember your spouse being insulting toward you in these kinds of ways, please do not presume that he was just having a bad day. Just the fact that he said anything, is a good indication that he had issues on his mind, and in his own thought life, he is turning over, and mulling over how he feels, and what to do about it.

Think about any of those events that you can remember, and maybe jot them down. You might begin to see a pattern, and then can develop an insight that you did not have before.

OBSERVE:

If you have stepped back and can now see the signs that your relationship had been cracking for some time, you should now try to observe what is happening with your partner at this time. Has he been unfaithful? Has he admitted infidelity, but assured you that it is all over? Has he denied any outside interests, but is threatening to leave because he just needs some space?

These are all signs of what might be coming down the road toward you. He may have told you that he is not happy, but then he doesn't go. If that is the case, then you have an opportunity to learn what is going on by his behavior. Maybe he really wants to leave you, but he doesn't know what will happen to the children. Maybe he doesn't want to lose everything and ruin his finances.

By observing his behavior and concentrating on what he says to you, and even what he does not say to you, you can begin to figure out what may happen to your relationship. The important thing here is for you to step back and take stock and OBSERVE.

Whatever you do, DO NOT PROD HIM FOR INFORMATION. One of the things we like to do as human beings is to ask lots of questions.

Please resist the urge to do so. Sometimes, he is working through is own unhappiness, and you can push him over the brink by asking him where he has been, who was he with, what has he been doing, and other nagging-type of questions.

Additionally, such an inquisition can make you seem desperate and militant. It is better for you if you just quietly observe. Maybe even start a small notebook, noting anything unusual that you have noticed.

One lady commented that after she left for work in the morning, her daughter noticed that the phone light came on in the daughter's bedroom extension. The husband was clearly calling someone in the morning after the wife left for work, and the daughter just casually mentioned "Why does daddy call someone every morning?"

That information was helpful to that partner in identifying that she was not at fault for the rift in the relationship, but that daddy had found an outside interest.

TAKE STOCK:

It may be more devastating than you can imagine learning that your loved one has been unfaithful, but this is where you need to go, before you consider your options. Don't worry about what he has or has not done.

Taking stock is about YOU. The process of observing and of taking stock are somewhat iterative. You will go back and forth again and again. You learn a piece of information, and then you evaluate that information based on how YOU feel about the news.

For example, you may learn that your partner has been meeting someone for lunch every Wednesday or every Friday. This is a fact you have learned through observation. Maybe you noticed a credit card receipt for regular lunches that seemed a little high for one person. Maybe a friend noted that she saw your husband at lunch with a female.

Whatever the information happens to be, you then take stock of how you feel about that information.

You might be crushed to even think that your partner would deceive you–even if the matter went no further than lunch. You might not care that he has lunch with a female. Or you might be so indignant that your partner is lying to you, that you really are fed up with him yourself, and you don't care what else he does.

By observing and taking stock, you begin to find a new reality about your relationship. Once you thought your relationship was one thing, and now you have begun to reengineer your relationship--in your mind–to be something more like what it actually is.

Please be reminded that this process of observing–or snooping as some have called it–may bring information to you that you don't want to know.

If you are not ready to probe yet, then just sit back and wait until your curiosity overcomes your fear. At some point in the first ninety days, you will begin to want to know what is at the bottom of your partner's changed behavior.

If he has left, it will be more difficult to observe in day-to-day settings, but at least if he has left, your breakup will become known, and you will not be pretending everything is fine, while at the same time trying to gather information.

In fact, if he has left, you may get an avalanche of calls and visits from friends letting you know that he has been spotted and what he is doing out there.

In any case, now is the time to keep your COOL. You have discovered a crack in the dike, and now you will need to determine if it can be repaired, rebuilt, or scrapped altogether.

FIVE

DON'T

DO ANYTHING DRASTIC!!!

Sometimes a partner does such an effective job of blaming his spouse that she is the cause of the split, that she sinks into a depression so great that she begins to think that it would be better for everyone to just get out of the way and make the ultimate sacrifice to give everyone else the gift of happiness. If you are thinking about ending it all, taking an overdose of something, putting a gun to your head, driving into a tree, or in some other way harming yourself STOP IT!!!

There is only ONE thing to say about that:

Don't DO ANYTHING desperate WHEN you are desperate!!!

Desperation is the WORST time for desperate acts. They just seem to feed themselves, and everything just keeps getting worse.

You might feel that maybe the children would be better off with your husband than with you or maybe you have been convinced that you really are to blame for all your troubles. You might be thinking that if you just "went away", that everything will be fine for all of those whom you love.

Again, just STOP IT!!!

You are struggling with a situation where your partner has just DUMPED YOU. How wonderful will he be to YOUR children when you are no longer around?

Do you want your children dragged from girlfriend to girlfriend by your unfaithful husband?

Do you think you children will really be happier without you?

No, you need to maintain your own lifestyle and sanity and continue to care for your children and for yourself.

Of course, that is a really-tall order. At this time, depression can be very real. It can be like a heavy, black, wet blanket wrapped entirely around you. Even on the brightest summer day, you may not even see a glimpse of daylight. At those times, it is easy to think about getting it over with.

Please, please, please go to your calendar and look at where you are on your ninety-day countdown.

Dos and Don'ts When You've Been Dumped

You promised yourself that you would wait ninety days to see how you would feel then. Even if today is a really bad day, remember that many times, when you are plodding along in a funk, that it is then that suddenly you might get a great job offer, or a house you have been wanting to rent comes available, or one of the kids gives you a big hug, and tells you how much he loves you.

These are the times, when you will be thankful that you didn't do anything desperate in your desperate situation.

Maybe it is too hard for you. Maybe you just cannot get through this day. If you just cannot shake off feelings of destruction and depression, go to a friend–a trusted confidant–and tell her what you are thinking. Make sure that your friend is someone NOT defending your loveless partner but sees it from YOUR side. If you find that by talking through things, you can begin to feel better, then keep talking, but if you think you are still sinking deeper and deeper into depression and doom, then find someone to counsel with you.

Many public agencies and even churches have counseling centers where you can go to get help, and people professionally trained in helping you, can be a lifeline for your mind and spirit.

Why are you so depressed anyway? Why aren't you just plain MAD? Why are you sinking further and further into gloom and doom?

You might be surprised to know that many times, we get depressed when we feel that we are TRAPPED.

You have been left with all the responsibilities and burdens, but none of the perks. You have invested a good portion of your life in your partner. You have shared finances, shared children, shared an entire life.

Now he wants to take his marbles and go home. That leaves you trapped. Maybe you worked him through school, and you do not have enough education yourself to get a good job. Maybe you have small children to care for. Maybe your bills are high, and you don't know how you will make ends meet.

Please know that escaping through desperate acts will not make things better. You might be unsuccessful and end up harming yourself physically. You will surely have trouble with child custody. Even if you are successful at harming yourself, you will leave behind tragedy that those who love you will have to bear for their entire lives.

Also, if you think you will be punishing your partner, perish the thought. He may have a pang or two of guilt, but more likely, you will have given him a justifiable reason for his behavior. He will be able to say that you were always a desperate and needy woman with lots of problems.

No, the best thing that you can do when you are desperate, is to do nothing. It is better to just stop and think about things for awhile. If you do nothing, it is better than doing something that you will not be able to undo.

Remember that life is indeed worth living. Remember that just around the next corner may be an answer to your

Dos and Don'ts When You've Been Dumped

prayer. Think of this time in your life as being like an adventure.

You have had set before you a maze. You are solving the biggest crossword puzzle of your life. Sure, your happy life has been turned upside down, but maybe it was not really all that happy for you either. Maybe this interlude will give you an opportunity to see yourself clearly without looking through his lens. Sometimes out of a maze comes a world of other options.

It will soon become time to concentrate on YOU, and to learn what is best for YOU.

SIX

DO

KNOW YOUR OPTIONS

A fter hearing the worst possible news, and after taking the time to observe and think through the situation, now is a good time to begin to figure out your options.

The one question you should ask yourself is "How bad is it really, and what are my options?"

Naturally if you are facing a break-up in your home, it seems really pretty bad. What could be worse? But many people have gone through breakups, with positive results.

Consider some outcomes: Maybe this time apart will make your spouse realize what he really had with you, and he will have a renewed sense of commitment to you.

Maybe you will realize that your life was not perfect, and that you often felt demeaned, unappreciated, and used. This might be a good time for you to reevaluate how you feel about yourself, and how you expect to be treated.

Take a moment and consider what is the worst thing that can happen? You lose the house, car, your credit is ruined, and you struggle to make ends meet for you and the children.

While that does sound bleak, think about it for a moment. You can probably rent a decent apartment or side-by-side house in most areas of the country for around $850 per month. You can buy a decent used car for under $10,000 on a payment plan. You could get supplemental income from assistance agencies to help with groceries, rent, healthcare and other living expenses.

OH, WAIT A MINUTE you say. I would never accept welfare.

Well, let's be sensible here by saying that if the worst thing that happens is that you might need some public assistance, AND it is available to you, then it may not be that bad of a scenario. It is certainly better than depression, drugs, or suicide.

Also, you should bear in mind that most of us work all our lives, and pay taxes, and never ask for help from anyone. We have indeed contributed to the system all that time, so why should we feel embarrassed to ask for help when we are the ones who need it?

Dos and Don'ts When You've Been Dumped

Many women get help with daycare, college assistance, and other family expenses, and begin new lives all over again.

Maybe you already have a good, job, and this split-up will be more of an emotional trauma than a financial disaster.

Remember that you were single when you entered this relationship, and if you are single when you leave it, you will still be YOU. You say, I am 20 years older, I am 20 lbs heaver, and I have given this man the best years of my life.

For that, there should be a price to pay. He may need to pay child support and alimony. He may lose the house and the cars. Don't worry about HIM right now though. The important thing here is to figure out what YOU need to do to survive and be whole again.

Take some time to sit down and figure out what resources you will need to continue in your current lifestyle, and if you can swing it with just some minor changes, then you will have confidence that you can get through anything.

If you find that you will need to sell the house, or let the cars go, or make other big sacrifices, then by examining your options, you will be more prepared to face your new reality once you have considered the outcomes.

The important thing for you to do, is to examine your options, and more importantly, remember that you do have options.

If you can think of the worst possible scenario, and you can accept that as a possible new reality for you, then you will not be living in fear of the unknown.

If you can have an attitude, of "Oh well, I will do whatever I need to do for the children and myself", then you will be in control of your own destiny. He will no longer own and control you.

One of the unfortunate outcomes of a partner being dumped, is the feeling of helplessness. Once you realize that you are strong, capable, and can conceive any number of multiple options for how you will live and get through this difficult time, you will begin to have confidence. Also, your partner will begin to see you as less desperate and less needy, and this may open up some opportunity to work through issues that caused the split.

SEVEN

DON'T

GET EVEN!!!

There was movie that was done a few years back about a woman who was married to an attorney in California, who was dumped by her husband. In desperation, she took a gun and went over to the home of her ex-husband and his new (young) wife, and she shot and killed them both.

There were cheers from many a dumped wife in this country when that movie was shown, but the fact is that the husband won out in the end. His unacceptable behavior led to his wife's increasingly bad behavior until she finally took the ultimate action, and now she will spend the rest of her life in prison.

They had four children, and the children became virtually orphaned. Their father is dead, and their mother went to prison. This was not a good outcome.

Why is it that getting even is such a bad idea? Won't it make the offended partner feel better? Why shouldn't the rat eat some of his own poison?

Let us examine some ways that the offended partner tries to get even, and let's see the likely result.

BERATING YOUR CHILDREN'S FATHER TO THEM:

This is a VERY COMMON behavior in women who have been dumped. Naturally, the woman is hurt, and under the circumstances she begins her tell-all behavior to her children. She berates their father. She tells them how he abandoned THEM, and how much he hates her and how little he loves THEM. Her children are literally TRAPPED with her. They are either in her home being bombarded with her hateful and bitter charges, or they are with him, sometimes secretly hating him themselves, for how unhappy he has made their mother.

Remember that you are not the only unhappy person in your breakup. Your children (his children) love both of you. You are their lives. They depend on you and on him. You are a family–the only family they have, and they take much of their own self-esteem from the soundness of their home and family.

Dos and Don'ts When You've Been Dumped

In shattering their image of their father, and of his love for them, you are shattering their own self image. If they think that life will never be good for them again, if they think THEY are unloved or unlovable, they will begin to feel desperate, and they will do desperate things. By ripping apart their father, you may be setting into motion events which you may be unable to stop.

Children of separation and divorce frequently act out in such ways, as drugs, alcohol, sex, and violence. At the very least, they will encounter poor eating and sleeping habits, and their grades will suffer.

It is YOUR job to ensure THEIR well-being, by encouraging them that everything will work out, and that both you and their father love them. You might tell them that their father has lost his way, and encourage them to support him perhaps in deeds, prayers, and kindness. Talk about getting even. Here you will be getting WAY AHEAD. Your children will thank you for the rest of their lives for sustaining them through this dreadful ordeal.

RUNAWAY SPENDING:

Closing the credit cards may not be the first thing that your wayward husband thinks of doing when he picks up and leaves. There may be a lot of open credit that you can use.

You might think that you are getting even by spending every credit card to the maximum limit. You might think that by ruining his credit that you will ruin him.

Let's think about that one too. It might be better for you to remove your name from any credit that HE HAS since he may be spending up to the limit as well. You may even want to cancel any credit that you and he share together. You would want to keep any credit that is in your name only, and you will want to protect your credit.

By ruining his and your credit, you will be digging yourself into a deep hole that may take years to climb up from.

The best thing that you can do is to spend your money very carefully. If you go to court and can prove that you were careful in using your resources, you will again be WAY AHEAD. Nobody will respect you if you try to ruin yourself and HIM.

Threatening Him and His Girlfriend:

First off, he has already made a big mess of his life and has already embarrassed himself by maybe running around with a girl half his age. While he thinks he has hit the jackpot, everyone else is laughing behind his back.

Everyone knows what a trophy wife or a trophy girlfriend is all about. Everyone knows that such dependence on young women is the sure sign that an older man has lost his confidence, and his own self-esteem. He needs the assurance from the next generation that he is relevant.

He is the only one who seems not to know or understand that the reason this young thing is interested in him, is the same reason that his wife is interested in him

Dos and Don'ts When You've Been Dumped

—because he is a wonderful husband, father, provider and family man.

The problem is that he is not ANY OF THOSE THINGS to the new girlfriend. As soon as he disengages from his wife and family, he is just another loose cannon of a man on the prowl.

The offended wife does not need to threaten him or his girlfriend. The offended wife only needs to protect her own (and her children's own) interests in her marriage and let him work out his illegitimate relationship.

Others will see him for what he is. If his girlfriend sees a tug-of-war beginning between her and his wife, she will be all-the-more smitten with him.

Better that you just tell him that he may not have a girlfriend and still live with you. You have dignity and value and will not be humiliated by his bad behavior. Remember, it is NOT YOUR FAULT. Do not own his bad behavior. However, do not create bad behavior of your own.

One other thing about threatening him or his girlfriend(s)—it may be ILLEGAL. The line between hurtful speech and behavior and hateful speech and behavior is not a bright line, and you may not realize that you have crossed it.

He may be a mean enough scoundrel to bait you into behaving badly yourself. DO NOT participate in ANY WAY in any illegal behavior. Remember to keep your COOL. If you find that you are losing control of your emotions, take a bath, watch a movie, take a nap, ANYTHING. Just do not act out. You will be giving him ammunition to use against you later. Again, keep your COOL, and you will be WAY AHEAD.

There are other ways that you might think of to get even. You could burn his clothes–you could go to his work and make a scene–you could stalk him–you could hit, bite and kick him. Really, the list of bad things that you could do is endless. And while you might think you are getting even, you are really, only doing bad things.

Just like he is embarrassing himself by his bad behavior, you will only be hurting yourself and your children by acting out your own bad behavior.

You will be WAY AHEAD (not just even) if you maintain dignity, decorum, and class.

EIGHT

DO

BE KIND—IT'S GOOD FOR YOU

It might seem odd to you that you should be asked to DO this one.

Being kind is probably the last thing on your "to do" list right now. Your life is being torn apart by this unappreciative man. He is trying to destroy you, your children, and your way of life, and here is a recommendation to you that you be kind.

First off, there is great benefit to you in being kind to yourself. You need to take the time to shower, apply makeup, do your hair, and in general keep your appearance clean and healthy.

Of course, there are some nights when you don't sleep a wink. You toss and turn, and cry. You have nightmares, and when you awake, you are never sure if you had a nightmare, or if you are really living a nightmare.

It is easy to let your personal care and good health slip away. You might be finding yourself skipping meals, and in some cases both you and your children are missing meals.

In a way, you might feel that you don't deserve kindness. Your reason for existence has just dumped you, and maybe he is right, maybe you don't deserve a good life. Maybe you don't deserve him.

Once again, just STOP IT!!!

Your kindness to yourself is a reward in and of itself. If possible, continue life as you always lived it. Your children will suffer much less disruption. They will see your gentle side, and your home will be warm and safe.

You may also discover an interesting phenomenon. People will begin asking you for advice on how to handle their problems.

As others observe the grace with which you are dealing with your own personal disaster, they will begin to share with you their problems. They will begin to see you as somewhat of an expert on marriage, breakups, and home life, and will look to you for guidance.

You will find that if you are kind to yourself, and to them, that you might find encouragement in your own encouragement to others.

Sometimes the truth never sounds so true as when it is uttered from your own mouth.

Dos and Don'ts When You've Been Dumped

When you find yourself telling others not to demean their own loved one, you will see the wisdom in your own good behavior throughout your ordeal.

To reestablish your good self-esteem, you might also try an exercise program at the local recreation center, or maybe plan to go to a movie once every couple of weeks with a trusted friend.

It may have been years since you did anything without your spouse, but now you are treating yourself to the movies that YOU like to watch, and you are wearing the makeup and hairstyle that you think enhances your beauty.

Being kind to yourself is a reward that you will want to give to yourself for all the stress and sacrifice that you have endured.

You can be perfectly frugal in how you spend your time and your money. Being kind to yourself is not an indulgence, it is a foundation block for you to build back some of the YOU that you have lost.

NINE

DON'T

SIGN ANYTHING!!!

You have just been told that you were never loved. You are to blame for his lifetime of unhappiness, and that he needs some time and space. Or maybe you found out about another woman or found incriminating information about his "hidden" life.

You are in a panic. How will you survive? How will you pay the bills? Will the children and you lose your hospitalization? Will you lose your home, your car? How are you going to manage?

Maybe you confronted him, maybe he confessed. Whatever happened, you are in a tailspin.

After you have wandered through days of depression and confusion, he comes to you with a document that he asks you to sign. He tells you that he promises to take care of you and his children for the rest of their childhood, if only you will sign this document.

You stare at the words. They seem to say that you are releasing him from your marriage. He is asking you to sign away your marriage.

And for this, he promises to take care of you. You are so afraid of what will happen, that you begin to relent. He is so nice right now. He hasn't been this nice in weeks. He is telling you that he loves his children, and wants to do what is best for them, and for you. What should you do?

STOP RIGHT THERE!!!

Think about that for a moment. Here he is asking you to sign away your marriage, and for that, he is promising to take care of you. Really now, if he truly wanted to take care of you, and if his children were his greatest concern, then why would you need to sign anything? Why isn't he living in your home, under your roof, and caring for you and his family as he has always done in the past?

If you think that by signing this document, that all will somehow fall back into place, please be aware that this is probably another of his TRICKS.

Generally, it is not the best advice that women run to an attorney at the first whiff of trouble. It is always possible, that your partner has just lost his way or is having

Dos and Don'ts When You've Been Dumped

problems at work, or is unhappy with aging, or any number of things, and maybe he can pull himself back together again.

However, when he begins to bring or send documents to you, or if there is ANY hint of lawyer involvement from his side, then it is definitely time for you to seek legal counsel on your side.

Even before you look for an attorney, remember DON'T sign anything.

Think about it for a moment. Here he is making these promises to take care of his family, but what is he really doing? He is living someplace else, possibly with someone else, and he is trying to disengage himself from you AND his family.

There is nothing that he can promise you, that you don't already own.

You already are married. Marriage is a contract. You have rights under your marriage contract. You own property together, you share in his social security benefits, you already have custody of your children. You are the legitimate partner of this man, and anything that you sign under duress will only limit your rights, not expand them.

No, if he comes to you with papers, make it your business to find an attorney.

Maybe you are thinking that you cannot afford an attorney. The truth is that you cannot afford not to have an attorney. You will be able to find attorneys in your local directories, and many of them provide a free first consultation. If you explain your circumstances, both financial and relationship problems, they will be able to guide you.

There may be resources available to you through a legal defense fund, or social services to help you with the cost of defending yourself.

It might be good that you find an attorney who represents women in these matters. There are fine attorneys who understand the impact on the WIFE when she has been dumped. Remember, you have the interests of your family resting on your shoulders, and you need to have someone who will help you protect those interests and protect your family.

Also, it might be best that YOU DO NOT, begin divorce proceedings unless divorce is something that you really WANT. You might just want to sit back and see how things play out. He may find that his trophy woman turns out to be a demanding, whining baby who is "at him" all the time for favors and rewards. In a little while, he may begin to realize how good he had it when he was living with you and his family. He may NEVER divorce you.

If he does begin divorce proceedings however, you will want to have your affairs in order, and may even want to contest the divorce.

This is the reason that you SHOULD NOT SIGN ANYTHING he asks you to sign. If you end up in court, you want to be the one on the high moral ground with your affairs in order, with your home and children in order,

Dos and Don'ts When You've Been Dumped

and with no "signed-away" rights for him to use as leverage.

You do not want to be the one explaining yourself or your behavior. Remember that he is the one behaving badly. You are the abandoned and injured wife and mother who is the voice of reason in this otherwise devastated relationship.

TEN

DO

BE OKAY (FOR YOU AND YOUR CHILDREN)

If you are feeling that your life is totally out of control, this is THE ONE area where you have the MOST control.

You have been abandoned and you feel trapped. Think for a moment how trapped your children feel. In addition to having their father leave, are they also left with a hysterical, depressed mother?

There is an old saying that the children will be as okay as their mother is. You have TOTAL control of how your children perceive YOU.

It will not be easy. Remember, you cannot go around berating their father, and confiding in your children about your unhappiness, their shame, or any of the details of what is happening around them.

Instead you will need to carry on your daily activities as though nothing has changed. You might even need to sugarcoat some of the events that will take place. You will want to stay in your home for as long as possible, so you will not want to pack up and move unless or until it is necessary.

Non payment of the mortgage will affect both of you, but if you cannot pay the mortgage, and he does not pay it, you can try to agree on selling the house, and then while it is being marketed, you can make it fun for you and the children to look at apartments, or houses to rent.

Also, you should continue to participate in activities as before. If the children play sports, continue going to their games. Continue to be friendly and composed around the other parents. Remember, you are not the one behaving badly, so don't be embarrassed by your husband's absence. You do not need to explain yourself, or his absence.

Also, try to prepare meals as before. You are STILL a family, and if your children see that you are unfazed by what is going on, they will be less concerned, and more contented.

It is bad enough that their father is absent–they realize it and feel his absence. But if they know that you are there and will guard their interests, then they will not worry about themselves or you.

Dos and Don'ts When You've Been Dumped

Please be reminded again of things you should NOT do:

Do not cry in the presence of your children.
Do not berate their father to them.
Do not drink or do drugs.
Do not bring other men into your home.
Do not become violent or hysterical.

And again, following are helpful things that you should DO:

Make regular meals.
Do regular laundry and cleaning.
Be engaged in your children's lives (school and activities).
Stay on the best budget possible.
Be as positive as you can be.

You might be saying "Come on now, do I look like superwoman?"

To that you should know that while you may not look like her, you should certainly ACT like her. It doesn't matter how bad you feel, it only matters how bad your children SEE that you feel. This may be the hardest part of this whole breakup, but it is the ONE PART THAT YOU CONTROL.

You are in total control of your own behavior and your own response to this catastrophe, and if you ACT like everything is going to be okay, then your children will believe you and believe in you. And surprisingly, much of the outcome will be better than you think.

If you can come through this experience with healthy children and a healthy YOU, you will be far better off than women who have destroyed themselves and their families in the process.

Once again remember, YOUR CHILDREN will be OKAY if YOU ARE OKAY!!!

ELEVEN

DON'T

LET IT EVER HAPPEN AGAIN

What?

Are you to blame? After all these dos and don'ts, is the suggestion here that you are the one that has caused this to happen?

NO. Everyone knows that you did not cause this breakup. While you and he have both made some mistakes along the way, you are not responsible for this miserable breakup.

Probably nobody really knows exactly what caused it. Maybe it was his poor self-esteem. Maybe he wanted more excitement in his life. Maybe he is just a big jerk who wants to dump all his responsibilities and be a child again. The point here though is that it doesn't really matter what HE DID or even what HE DOES.

What matters right now, is YOU and what has happened to YOU.

What has happened to you is that you were going along living your life, doing your day-to-day activities, possibly happy and content, totally unaware that a tsunami was about to hit, and then WHAM, you were hanging on for your life.

The one factor that made this whole experience such a disaster in your life was the SHOCK factor.

And THAT is what you never need to let happen again.

A catastrophe is really, only a catastrophe if we are unprepared for it. If there is a storm, and there is a shortage of food, it is only a catastrophe if you do not have any food. If you have already planned ahead and stored up, then it is just an inconvenience.

If there is a fire, and you have a plan to escape the house, and you have your important papers protected, and you have insurance, it is just an inconvenience. Sure, you will cry and be unhappy, but you will recover MUCH quicker if you had planned FIRST for the fire, than to try to figure out what to do LATER.

If you lose your job, and you have a good resume, and you keep up your appearance, and training, and you live on a budget, and you have a little money saved, it is a big inconvenience. But if you have no plan and no options, it will be a big disaster the day you get your pink slip.

Dos and Don'ts When You've Been Dumped

There are many events in our lives that are DIFFICULT to endure, but what makes a bad experience MUCH WORSE, is the SHOCK factor.

When you have a family, you learn to depend on one another, and you trust that you will have help in times of trouble, but it is unwise to be oblivious to the possibility that your partner will not ALWAYS be there for you or will not ALWAYS be on YOUR side.

Smart women prepare for the unexpected as well as the expected.

In the future, make sure to maintain your own credit. You can have a credit card in your name only. Maybe you each should have separate credit cards. You will probably have both names on mortgages, but maybe you will want to title your cars so that each one of you owns your own car.

In matters of savings, maybe you will want to keep a small account that you contribute to regularly for unexpected emergencies. If all goes well, and your relationship lasts forever, then you have some "mad money" that you can use for a vacation, or some special treat later, but if you do have a disaster, you will have something to use in a pinch.

Also, have a plan of response if this partner (or maybe a different partner some place down the road), begins to waiver in his commitment to you. The best response is to not permit yourself to be dumped again. If you see that your partner is not committed to you, then you will be better prepared to deal with whatever begins to happen in your relationship.

Instead of wondering how you will survive, you might only need to decide when you will require him to leave.

Make sure that the ball is at least partly in YOUR court. You want to be loving, fair, and engaged, but you do not ever want to be needy again.

TWELVE

....

DO

BE PREPARED FOR YOUR MARRIAGE TO WORK!!!

Throughout this book, the focus has been on the crushing disappointment of your failed marriage. However, what if it begins to WORK???

What is your plan if your spouse decides that he has made a BIG mistake?

He does love you–doesn't even know why he ever thought he didn't. He wants to return to you and his children. He wants to make it up to you.

Maybe the picture is not that rosy. Maybe he is just willing to return to you. He is willing to try to make things work. He has assured you that he has broken it off with whomever else he was involved with, and he wants your marriage to work.

This will be the hardest challenge. Women ask themselves all the time, "How can I ever trust him again?"

The answer is that you will need to ONLY forgive him–it is YOURSELF whom you must TRUST.

It will be almost impossible to ever return to your pre-breakup state of total trust. Back then you never dreamed that he could betray you. Now, you can hardly believe that he will ever be faithful and trustworthy again. Now, even if he is not unfaithful (or maybe never was unfaithful), you still cannot bring yourself to trust in his love for you.

You must stop building your expectations around HIM and what HE will do, and instead, plan your life around what YOU will do.

The key to successful reconciliation is your PLAN. Remember that your life crumbled before your eyes for two reasons–the first was what he did or what he revealed to you–but the second was your total lack of preparation for anything but marital bliss.

Now YOU are different. You can go on because YOU have a plan. You can believe in YOU. You can believe in your ability to weather whatever storm comes along. You did it once, and while you are willing to give him this one more chance, you know that if it does not work out, that you can weather it again–one last time.

It will be his job to make sure that he does not give you any reason for suspicion. He needs to be where he is supposed to be doing what he is supposed to be doing.

Dos and Don'ts When You've Been Dumped

You must make it clear to him that you will not tolerate lies and deceit.

It should not be your plan, however, to follow him around and snoop into all his business. He is a man and an adult, and he should be treated with respect, even though he has not earned it. Consider it your gift to him if necessary, but do not belittle him or nag at him or constantly remind him of his past mistakes. Remember that regret will be hard for him to live with also.

He is trying to build back his reputation with his children, his friends and family, and with the community in general, and he will need your support to continue.

It may be that the other woman (if there was one) might not want to let go very easily. Make no mistake, however, he MUST let her go. He must dedicate himself to you and your family if the relationship is to work.

YOU are the key that will make that happen. If you are pouting around all the time, or crying, or reminding him of all his past mistakes, he will be unable to manage the regret and remorse, and he will want to leave just to get out of the discomfort zone that he has made for himself.

The best way to heal, is to consider every day that you are together as a family a GIFT. This is the only day that you get to live. Yesterday is gone, and tomorrow is promised to no one. You only get today.

Don't worry about what he will or will not do tomorrow. Plan this day and plan it well. Plan for fun. Go on picnics, go to the movies, go to the children's sports events, visit friends and family. Make your lives together as "normal" as possible–better even.

After a while, you will feel less rehearsed. You will begin to feel as happy as you are trying to feel. There may be times, when you get a nagging feeling that maybe he is NOT being totally honest.

You need to wait for the information to come to YOU. Maybe at first you will join him on trips to the hardware, or errands to the office. Maybe you will need that reassurance for a while. But sooner or later, you will need to let him go.

If he comes back, he is yours–if he does not come back, he was never yours.

THIS TIME, however, you have a plan. You know what you will be doing for the rest of your life. With or without him, you will be a happy well-adjusted person with hopes, and dreams, and plans for yourself.

You will want to be perfectly clear with him that this is not a game. Your relationship will not be a yo-yo with constant going back and forth between you and somebody else.

If you find out that he is betraying you, then the marriage is over. Do not put him on probation though. The marriage is on firm footing from day one. But it will be over any time (tomorrow or 10 years from now) if he betrays your trust again.

That is how you get past the past. You live in the day and look forward to your future.

Dos and Don'ts When You've Been Dumped

Whether you stay together or go your separate ways, you will learn that, over time, you will be okay. If you do not implode in the early days of this crisis, you will move on to other better days.

If you follow these dos and don'ts, you might find that you are a stronger, more capable, and well-adjusted person than you have ever been before.

ABOUT THE AUTHOR

This creative author grew up in a challenging and scary world. She learned early that her life would require faith and courage to survive and to overcome life's obstacles. Over the years, she reached many milestones in her own life including teaching college, writing for a large city newspaper, and providing analytical support to multiple major corporations. Her books "No Ashes for Me", "Dos and Don'ts when You've Been Dumped", and "Nobody NEEDS to be FAT Anymore", are written as helpful resources designed to inspire her readers in overcoming their own life's challenges and in reaching toward their own happiness and satisfaction.

www.ingramcontent.com/pod-product-compliance
Lightning Source LLC
Chambersburg PA
CBHW020430010526
44118CB00010B/509